WOW!
CAN WE DO THAT AGAIN?

All Time Favorite
Quick and Easy
Science Experiments
You Can Do at Home

compiled by Jim Erskine
Illustrated by Jess Erskine

Rolling Donut Press

THANKS TO OUR CONTRIBUTORS!

We wish to thank our friends & readers who contributed their own experiments for this collection:

Mandy Blackmon, Scott Alan Blanchard, Jennifer Blake, Bruce Boehne, Deborah Cariker, Lyn Carradine, Creation Academy, Kim Dickey, Rose-Marie Gallagher, Jodi Galland, Cindy Gould, Dawn Griffith, Jennifer Hartnagle, Jennifer Koontz, Laurie Kroeker, Heather Matson, Sue Moisiadis, Elizabeth Nickel, Kimmie Olson, Rachel Q, Christy Patterson, Georgi Persons, Abby Rawlins, Cara Riggles, the Schaefer family, Amy Shattuck, Shannon Sims, Michelle Stansell, Karen Steele, Joanne Stein, Lisa Sutton, Rebekah Trusty, Jennifer Walker, Heather Wiegand, Brandy Whitmer ...plus many others who also contributed similar ideas & suggestions. This volume would not be nearly as good as it is without your input and participation! thank you so much! we appreciate you!

WOW!
Can We Do That Again?

Introduction

Kids are just naturally curious & full of questions. They love to learn, and "hands on" experiments at home or in a group activity is a great way to get them excited about science.

That's what this collection is all about: Sparking a love of science and having fun in the process. There are dozens of wonderful, exciting experiments in this manual – They are simple, easy to do, and fun for students of all ages. And many of them are "all time favorites" of other families.

Our mascots Rusty, Ben and Penny are tagging along for the ride since they love science, and want to make it more fun and appealing for younger students. Don't worry – they've promised to stay out of your way and not make too big a mess behind them!

A few quick suggestions from us to you as you jump in to this collection:

Most of these experiments are great for all ages, with age-appropriate supervision. Just use your judgment. Every one of these has proven to be a kid-favorite, so it will be hard to go wrong with any of them.

We believe that a good science experiment doesn't have to be a small part of an overwhelming "lesson plan" to be a successful learning experience. Just the simple science activity all by itself is a great way to encourage curiosity and learning. So let us encourage you NOT to overdo the academics with these experiments. Too much "lesson time" and explanation surrounding the activities can suck the excitement right out of your students, and they may quickly lose interest in learning anything further about the subject.

The goal with these experiments is not to learn everything there is to know about a subject. (that can come later!) The goal is to have fun and encourage curiosity.

Lead but don't push! Let your kids take ownership of the activity and try to figure out the answers for themselves. Ask questions about the experiments, but take your time about giving away the answers. Give them a chance to think about it before explaining the "whys" and "hows" of why the experiments work. Questions like: "What do you think will happen when we do this?" or "What do you think would happen if we did it this way instead?" will get them thinking it through on their own. Just be an audience for your kids' experiments and encourage them as they think things through. Ask good leading questions so they can verbalize back to you what is happening, and why. If they can do that, they are learning.

Let the kids make mistakes. Not every science experiment will turn out perfect. You should let your kids know that it's okay if they mess it up. use any mistakes or problems that occur as a learning experience. Often scientific discoveries have been made by accident and trial and error. Ask questions: "Why do you think that happened?" or "What could you do different next time?"

Don't limit your science experimenting to any specific subject that you are currently studying. curiosity knows no bounds. Different types of experiments and activities often open whole new fields of exploration & learning for your kids. Even though they may not learn about a subject "in-depth" right now, a memorable demonstration will definitely stay with them, and will likely resurface later when you are studying other science concepts.

We hope you will have fun with these family-proven favorite experiments and activities, and they give your kids lots of opportunities to play "scientist" and do a bunch of "hands on" experimenting of their own. In the process, you'll spark their love of learning... and you'll also create some of their favorite memories for years to come!

A Few Safety Tips:

In a science laboratory, students are often required to wear lab coats to protect their clothes (and themselves) from spills or stains. When doing some potentially messy experiments at home, encourage your kids to wear their own "lab coat" or apron to keep from getting dirty.

Safety goggles protect eyes from getting splattered or affected by any gas, liquid or objects that might be used in a given experiment. Wear goggles when appropriate for any home science experiments!

Messes will happen! Lots of these experiments can be messy, so be prepared for that and allow it to happen. Students should be involved in the clean up time as well as the experiments. Make sure your experiments are conducted in an appropriate space – indoors or outdoors - and the tools to clean up and put away materials are provided.

Plan ahead! Know what supplies are needed and what needs to be done before beginning any experiment. This will help in locating and setting up your working area, and also helps your students focus on the actual activity.

Kids should always get permission from their parents to perform any of these experiments. Not only is this a safety matter, but it is always best to have someone on hand as an audience for your experiments, to talk about it, and to consult instructions when needed.

Have fun!

Climbing Water!

Here is a science experiment we did earlier this year that was the biggest hit!

Needed:

a clear glass pie plate
a votive candle in its holder
a jar
water (color it blue with food coloring if desired)

What to do:

We lit the candle, put the jar over and watched. As the candle burned all the oxygen in the jar….

The flame went out and then…..

The water crept up into the jar!

I explained that the flame needed oxygen to burn, and when the oxygen runs out the jar has a partial vacuum in it and the water rushes inside to fill that space.

I think we did this 5 or 6 times. The kids loved it!

- Dawn Griffith

The Instant Science Diet!

Here's another cool experiment that is similar to the "climbing water" experiment... but does it in a most unusual way. It just takes a "BRAVE" volunteer !

Needed:
1 16 oz glass
1 piece of white bread
2 matches
1 volunteer to "lose weight" - preferably someone who has a little extra tummy.

What to do:
1. The volunteer lies on his or her back with tummy exposed. <insert evil laugh>
2. Wet the bread a little and smash it flat, then lay it on the volunteer's tummy. <yuck!>
3. Take one match and stick it into the bread, head up as if it were a candle.
4. Have the glass ready to quickly place over the match when ready.
5. Light the second match and use it to light the match sticking out of the bread.
6. Immediately place the glass over the match on the volunteer's tummy, squishing its edge into the bread slightly (this creates a nice seal).
7. Watch the volunteer lose some tummy weight!
(The match burning in the glass creates a vacuum which pulls up the skin from the volunteer's tummy!)
- Cindy Gould

The Flame Tornado!

Take a recently-emptied bottle of rubbing alcohol, go in a dark room, and drop a lighted match into the bottle. (Make sure the bottle is empty!)

It will create a loud whooshing sound, cause a large cool-looking tornado-like flame, and then extinguish almost immediately.

This demonstrates combustion, a vacuum, and change in air pressure.

- Georgi Persons

The Amazing Egg in a Bottle !

We just did a series of "eggsperiments" on chicken eggs, and this one was considered incredibly cool, by both child and mother :).

Needed:

Peeled hard boiled eggs (you may have to try more than once)
matches or lighter
Paper scrap (a twisted piece of paper towel worked well)
A Bottle with opening slightly smaller than narrow part of egg (glass is preferable, but plastic worked. We used a single-serving Snapple iced tea bottle)

What you do:

1. Light paper scrap and toss into bottom of bottle - paper needs to stay alight
2. Quickly place narrow end of egg into neck of bottle.

3. When the flame goes out, the egg gets sucked into the bottle.

What this shows:

Burning the paper in the bottle consumes the oxygen in the bottle, creating a partial vacuum. As the air in the bottle cools the remaining air molecules move closer together, and the egg sinks down and seals the mouth of the bottle. The pressure outside the bottle is higher than that inside the bottle, which pushes the egg inside.

- Joanne Stein

Erupting Soda!

Needed:

1 Large bottle of soda (diet coke works best)

About ½ pack of Mentos candy

A home-made, or purchased, Geyser Tube & Toothpick

What To Do:

1. Make a home-made Geyser tube – roll a piece of card stock into a tube the same width as the mouth of the soda bottle.

2. Pierce the Geyser Tube with the tooth pick about 1 inch from the bottom – all the way through.

3. Carefully open the soda bottle (Don't shake bottle)

4. Gently place the Geyser Tube inside the mouth of the soda until the tooth pick is balanced on the top.

5. Gently place the Mentos inside the

Geyser Tube, until they are balanced on top of the tooth pick.

6. Put on your Safety Goggles.

7. Carefully pull out the toothpick, dropping the candy into the soda, and RUN!! The soda will shoot up to 20 feet in the air.

What is Happening?

Soda is bubbly because carbon dioxide (CO_2 is pumped in at the bottling plant. Some bubbles are released upon opening the soda (the sizzling sound). Even more bubbles are released when something is dropped into the soda, or it's poured into a cup. The candy is covered by hundreds of tiny dimples. This means even more bubbles are released. This reaction happens so fast the soda is powered up into the air by the amount of bubbles trying to escape all at once.

   – Shannon Sims

Rock Candy !

Needed:

A wooden skewer, clothespin, tall glass or jar, pot & stove

1 cup water

2-3 cups sugar

What To Do:

1. Clip the wooden skewer into the clothespin so that the skewer can hang down into the cup about 1 inch from the bottom

2. Remove the skew-clothespin and set aside

3. Pour water into the pot.

4. Get the help of an adult to help you bring the water to a boil.

5. With adult, add about ¼ cup of sugar into the boiling water, stirring until it dissolves.

6. Keep adding more and more sugar, each time stirring until it's dissolved, until no more will dissolve (takes a while!)

7. Set pot aside to cool for about 10 minutes.

8. Dip the skewer about ½ way into the cooling solution.

9. Set skewer hanging in the empty cup to cool.

10. Have adult help you carefully pour the solution into the glass.

11. Allow the glass to cool and set it in a place where it won't be disturbed. Wait about 3-7 days for candy to grow!

What is Happening?

When you mixed the water and sugar you made a "Super Saturated Solution". This means so much sugar was added that it wouldn't have mixed if both ingredients hadn't been very hot. As the water cools, the sugar "comes out" of the solution forming back into sugar crystals. These sugar crystals stick together on the skewer. The skewer acts as a 'seed' that the sugar crystals can grow on.

- Shannon Sims

Color Symphony!

Needed:

a flat tray (like a cookie sheet)

food coloring (at least 3 colors)

whole milk, liquid dish soap

What to do:

1. Carefully pour milk into the tray so that it just covers the bottom

2. Add about 6-8 drops of different colored food coloring onto the milk in different spots.

3. Add about 5 drops of dish soap onto the food coloring.

4. Watch the color show!

What is Happening? The colors come from the food coloring obviously. But why do they dance? The purpose of dish soap is to break down fat. It does this on dirty dishes by attacking the grease (another word for fat) left over from the food we eat. Fat is also found in whole milk. When you drop the liquid soap onto the tray, it tries to break down (tear apart) the fats in the milk. While it's doing this, the colors will move around on the tray!

Side Note: You can even test the differences between dish soaps to see if there is much of a difference between the cheaper or more expensive variety! (Dawn is awesome for this experiment, it will actually make a see through hole in the puddle of milk as it 'eats' the milk fats instantly).

Sink or Float?

Gather a large number and
wide variety of household
and garage items that
won't be ruined if they get
wet. Suggestions include:
produce, tin foil (both a
sheet and crumpled tightly
into a ball), spare change,
socks, pencils, rubber
bands, tupperware, balls of
all kinds, empty plastic
containers, pots and pans,
toothpicks, silverware, flip flops, etc. The more the better. If
you have a swimming pool, gather all these items next to it,
along with the kids. If you don't, fill the bathtub and gather
everyone and everything there, or use a big plastic kiddie
pool.

You'll want to discuss the ideas of weight, mass and
displacement. Basically, an object will float if it weighs less
than the water it displaces when sitting on the surface. This is
why giant ships can float - even though they are immensely
heavy, water is very heavy, too, so the water that has to move
out of the way to accommodate the body of the ship weighs
more than the ship - so it floats. (To demonstrate how heavy
water is, fill the bucket you use to mop the floors with water
and ask the kids to carry it around (outside!). Just a gallon or
two of water weighs quite a bit.)

Then you're going to toss each item you've collected into the pool/tub. But before you do, poll your kids - do you think it will sink or float, and why? Ask before every object you throw in. In the beginning, they'll just be guessing, especially if they're younger. But as you proceed through your pile, you'll be able to see their little brains working, trying to figure it out. Eventually, the kids will start suggesting other items to toss in, to see if they'll sink or float. Unless it's something that can't get wet, do it!

This is a great outdoor activity on a hot day. We easily spent an hour doing this, tossing stuff in and talking about why it sank or floated. And although we didn't use alot of fancy jargon to explain what was happening, I think that by the end they had a much better handle on what kinds of things sink and what kinds float.

- Jennifer Walker

Blubber Gloves !

Needed:

Vegetable Shortening

Ice water

Do your kiddos ever wonder why a Walrus doesn't need a fur coat while swimming in the Arctic waters? Well, who needs fur when you have a nice coating of blubber?

 To teach the kiddos about how blubber insulates body heat, first have them put one of their hands in a bowl of ice water. See how long they can withstand keeping their hands in the icy water. Then, have them take their hands out of the water and dry them off. Coat the same hand thickly with Vegetable Shortening. Have the kiddos put their coated hand back into the icy water, and they will be AMAZED that their hands don't even feel cold at all!

- Amber Hockman

Foaming Colors !

Needed:
styrofoam egg carton
vinegar
baking soda
food coloring

My kids (mostly preschool) love to combine art and science.
We take a waterproof egg carton and put a small amount of
baking soda in each hole. Then I give them 3 spill-proof cups
with vinegar and a different color food coloring in each cup.
They are given a plastic eyedropper (I bought 500 for 5$ from
a science supply house and am now set for life). They have a
blast adding squirts of food dyed vinegar to the baking soda

piles, watching the foam, then using a different color to mix different colors. All the ingredients are non-toxic if they decide to taste it, and the amounts used result in a relatively small mess. in the process my three year old can use the phrase "chemical reaction" in a complete sentence and tell anyone who will listen that it makes "carbon dioxide and purple".

- Elizabeth Nickel

Make Moon Craters!

Needed:

pie tin

flour

items to drop!

One of our all-time favorite experiments was learning about the creation of craters on the moon. We learned from our text that the impact of meteors, for example, caused the craters. Since the moon has no atmosphere, unlike the earth, the meteors do not burn up and are free to crash on the moon's surface thereby creating the crater.

To demonstrate this effect, we took a large pie tin OUTSIDE, filled it with flour, placed a chair next to it, and had each child stand upon the chair taking turns dropping things (marbles, rocks both large and

small, high bounce balls, etc.). Each time we removed the item, we observed the associated size of the crater, noting that they got bigger with larger objects and heavier weights We then dropped the same objects from atop a deck - a place much higher than the chair top - to observe the difference in crater size.

The kids LOVED the effect of the spreading flour as the objects hit the pan. This could be done inside with enough tarps to protect the floors and walls, but it IS one of the messiest experiments we've ever done, so I wouldn't advise the indoor version for the faint of heart or the neat freak!

- Amy Shattuck

Fruit Surgery !

We recently moved to a new home with peach and apple trees in the yard. When we began to see fruit on the trees, I decided it was time to learn about growing fruit. Armed with small children's books from the library about how apples and peaches grow, we trekked outside for science class. My 2nd and 3rd graders were so excited. We found all the parts of the plants the books talked about and just followed it page by page. We picked up peach pits and fruit that had fallen to the ground. We also plucked an apple on a stem and brought them all inside. We spent the next hour dissecting the sepal, ovary, core, etc. and looking at everything inside. When we finished this simple exercise, my daughter exclaimed, "Now that's what I call school!" We all loved it.

– Lisa Sutton

Gloop Power!

Needed:
corn starch
water
bowl
optional: food coloring

You just can't go wrong with "gloop"! It's not a solid or a liquid. How can that be? All you need to make it is corn starch, water, and a bowl to mix it in. You don't even need a spoon because gloop is much more fun to mix with your hands. Start with corn starch and add water slowly until the mixture has the consistency of honey. When it's just right, you can poke and prod it like a solid, but you can't stick your hand in and pick it up because it will liquefy. Try it and see. You'll agree it's brain-tickling fun!

To maximize your fun, don't let your kids in on the "trick" before you make it. Pour it onto a baking sheet and, as soon as they get close, smack your hand on the gloop! If you made it right, they won't get spattered. But they don't know that! If you didn't make it right, you'll have a messy kitchen! (You did test it first, right?)

- Cara Riggles

Magic Soap !

Needed:

ivory soap

dish

microwave oven

optional: food coloring

This is a quick and super fun science experiment about air.

Cut an ivory soap bar into quarters. Use just one for now and set the rest aside. You will want to do this experiment again and again.

Now... put the piece of cut soap onto a small microwave safe dish. Put the soap and dish into the microwave. Set the microwave for 2 minute. Close the door of the oven and watch.... it happens fast. And it will not take the full time.

The soap will expand quickly, and becomes like fluffy clouds. why? Ivory soap is whipped with air. (thats why it floats) When heated , the molecules of water and air expand pushing the soap out into its new fluffy shape.

That's it... fast, fun and to the point. - Rebekah Trusty

EXTRA IDEA:

As an added bonus after it dries we crumble it up and add it with a few tablespoons of water and blend it until it turns to a yogurt consistency, then add some food coloring and put it into a ziploc bag, with a corner cut off, and we have instant bath paint, for the littler students. The kids beg to watch it "explode" over and over, and since it's easy and doesn't make a mess, mom is willing!

 - Abby Rawlins

Popsicle House Fever!

Using popsicle sticks, make 3 fairly similar houses. Size doesn't matter, but ours were about 6 inches on each side, with a roof. Paint the outside of one white, another black and the third one any other color or leave it plain. Attach a thermometer to an inside wall or under the roof of each one.

Record the temperature on each thermometer before beginning the experiment. Put all three houses in a sunny place, or a warm place in the shade. Leave them for 5 or 10 minutes, then quickly read the temperatures on each thermometer and record them.

How do the temperatures compare? Do you think the color of your clothing can help to keep you cooler on a hot day? Would the color of your clothing help to keep you warmer on a cool or cold day? Try this again in 6 months or another day when the temperature outside is significantly different from the first experiment and see how the outside temperature affects the results.

- Michelle Stansell

The Erupting Volcano!

Needed:

sand, clay, playdough, or other "building materials"

broom

vinegar

baking soda

I've used this science/geology/geography experiment over and over with my children, with co-op children, with children I was babysitting... and it never fails to get ooo's and aaahhh's!

You can utilize this hands-on activity while teaching about the Ancient World (Pompei) or about US geography and history

(Mount St. Helens), and about geology -- even the Flood!

This is an OUTSIDE activity, unless you just want lots of mess in your house! Using a sand and clay mix (stiff enough to "stand") or LOTS of play-doh, build a pyramid/mountain shape. The size is up to you, your work area, and your resources of clay/sand/play-doh. We usually make our model about 18 inches tall. Next, use a dowel rod or broom handle or stick to create a cylinder-shaped hole down the center of the mountain. Fill the hole with baking soda. Then, pour vinegar carefully into the hole/onto the vinegar -- and watch the volcano "blow".

For added fun, use building blocks, twigs, and plastic people to create villages and houses. You can also add red food dye to the vinegar before pouring it into the volcano so the "lava" is red.

- Deborah Cariker

Hovering Balloons !

Needed:

helium balloon
on a string

lego-type blocks

At the carnival,
each of our
young boys received a helium balloon. The string wasn't long
enough for them to retrieve the balloon from the ceiling on
their own, so we got out some legos to hook to the end of the
string and weight the balloons down. We tried various
combinations and sizes of bricks and attached the bricks
together normally, with the string between the two (or more)
bricks.

We were able to come up with a configuration for one balloon
that allowed the bricks to hover about 2 feet off the ground.
All of the other configurations and every configuration on the
other balloon either sank to the floor or floated to the ceiling.
My 4 and 6 year-old spent a good 20 minutes selecting brick
combinations and deciding whether to add or subtract bricks
and what size brick to use.

We talked about the properties of helium and also got around
to hot air balloons, why balloons and bubbles break... They
were full of related questions and we had a great time with
our challenge.   - Jodi Galland

Light up the Night!

This was hands down the favorite physics lab for my 5th grade son last year...

Needed:

D-cell battery
wooden spring style clothespin
24" x 12" piece of aluminum foil
flashlight bulb
masking tape or electrical tape
various materials to test, ie. paper, coins, rubber band, paper clip, etc.

Directions:

Fold the aluminum foil in half lengthwise 4 or 5 times to form a thin strip. Cut this into two 12 inch pieces and tape one end of each strip to opposite ends of the battery. Wrap the free end of one strip around the base of the flashlight bulb and clamp it in place with the clothespin. Using the clothespin as a handle, touch the metal tip of the bulb to the free end of the other foil strip. The bulb should light up because electrons can flow freely through the circuit.

You are now ready to test the materials you've gathered to see which ones will conduct electricity. Place the object to be tested on the free end of the foil strip and then touch the end of the bulb to the object. If the bulb lights up then the object is a conductor that is allowing electrons to move freely through the system to make a closed circuit. After testing a variety of objects, try to decide what the conductors have in common. (Note: All conductors are metal.)

To extend the activity, see if you can create housing for your light using lego style building blocks or other non-conductive materials. Keep the battery steady and try attaching the free end of the foil strip to a base piece. By using hinged pieces around the clothespin, you should be able to turn your light on by swinging the bulb into position to touch the foil and then turn the light off by pulling it away. Different colored cellophane or see through plastic covers can also be positioned above the bulb for interesting effects. Once you're satisfied with your creation, it can be used as a reading light at night.

- Lyn Carridine

Quick Cheese!

Needed:
2 1/2 gal milk, 2 c white vinegar
3 tsp baking soda, 3 tsp salt
2 Tbsp butter, 1/2 c sweet cream   Yield: 1 1/2 pounds

Easy, tasty & educational...vinegar cheese and quick cheese!
Cheese is always a great experiment. My 12 year old loves to
make it. It works with both raw and processed milk. This
recipe has the consistency of Velveeta, melts nicely, and tastes
good! This recipe dates back to the 1800's.

Heat milk to 128*F. Slowly pour in white vinegar, stirring all
the while, to sour the milk and create curds & whey. Kids love
this "magic" and you have just watched a chemical reaction!
Cover and let sit for 1 hour. Drain and work in baking soda
and salt with your hands (Kids love this too). Let sit 1/2 hour.
Congratulations! You just made *vinegar cheese.*

Eat it this way or to make it even better... Cut or tear into small
pieces (again...fun!). Melt butter in a saucepan and add sweet
cream. Stir, then add cheese pieces and melt over low heat.
Pour into your mold of choice.*

* I poured into a wide mouthed jelly jar as a mold. If you use
whole milk, it becomes a spreadable cheese, if you use skim,
you can slice it after loosening and removing it from its mold.

- Laurie Kroeker

Layers and Density!

We recently conducted a "kitchen" experiment that helps to explain the differences in density, mass, and volume. All that is needed in the experiment is:

a clear plastic or glass container
1/3 cup of vegetable oil
1/3 cup of water colored with food coloring
1/3 cup of liquid glycerin
beads, marbles, pieces if foam, and anything else your children want to test with!

Pour the glycerin into the bottom of the container, making sure that you do not touch the sides of the container. You will be layering the liquids and if the glycerin touches/runs down the side, it will cause the layers to mix instead of stacking.

Next, pour a layer of colored water into the container- allowing the water to run down the side of the container. If you pour the water into the glycerin, you will get a bubbly mess. Last, pour the vegetable oil into the container- allowing it to also run down the side of the container, completing the third layer.

Then, comes the fun! Allow the kids to form their hypothesis about whether the objects will float, sink, and which layer they will suspend in.

The explanation of the experiment is that each liquid has different density, meaning that even though the volume is the same for all three liquids, the mass for each is different. (Density = Mass / Volume) The higher the density of a substance, the more compact the substance. The glycerine is much denser than water, causing the water to float. The vegetable oil is less dense than the water, causing it to suspend at the top.

Questions for the kids: Why do some objects float and others sink? Which substance is the most dense?

Enjoy!!!

- Christy Patterson

Uniformity & Catastrophe!

This is a great geology experiment to see the difference between the principles of catastrophe and uniformity.

The experiment will demonstrate the principles of uniformity and catastrophe. In this context, the slow moving water will show how erosion and deposition can occur over time, and given large amounts of time, produce noticeable effects (uniformitarianism). It will also show that increasing water amount and velocity will produce far greater effects in less time (catastrophism).

Materials Needed:

Dirt piles or a garden bed, preferably bare dirt

Garden hose with running water

Camera or drawing paper and pencil

An irrigation pump or high pressure water supply would be helpful but not essential

Some Vocabulary to look up:

Principle of Catastrophe (catastrophism)

Principle of Uniformity (uniformitarianism)

Erosion

Deposition

Drainage channel

Meandering stream

Tributary

Sand bar

Stream bank

Delta

Velocity

Method:

1. It will be helpful to review the vocabulary before doing the experiment.

2. Using your garden hose, set up a slow moving water station on your dirt pile or bare patch. Start the water

running at a slow but steady velocity from the top of your pile or patch, and observe what happens.

3. The water will begin to erode the dirt and move it downhill, and given enough time, will form streams and drainage channels. Observe the shape of the streams formed and the locations of erosion and deposition. You may see tributaries, sand bars, deltas, and other forms associated with water.

4. Document your observations by drawing them or taking photos, so you can research the forms later.

5. Set up a fast moving water station, preferably on another dirt pile or patch. Turn up the velocity of the water and

observe what happens. Use the highest pressure possible. A thumb partially over the end of the hose will constrict the flow and get a good solid stream. The water will erode quickly and deposit large amounts of dirt elsewhere down the hill. Document what you observe with drawings or photographs.

6. Use the drawings and or photographs to make a lapbook, scrapbook, or report of your observations.

Conclusion:

Discuss how effective water is at moving things around. Point out that many land forms currently visible are made by slow moving water, and how some land forms could be made quite quickly given enough water at high velocity.

What We Actually Did

We had several huge dirt piles (10 feet high) in the side paddock due to some construction we were doing. We wanted to see the effect of water pressure on the piles of dirt, so we set up two stations.

The first station had running water coming out of the garden hose at low pressure. We set up the hose on top of a pile and turned on the water at low but steady pressure. The water made all sorts of lovely meandering streams as it ran down the pile. We looked at erosion, deposition, the shapes of drainage channels – lots of geology stuff. We even had a delta form at the base of the pile where the water hit level ground. The kids drew pictures of what they saw, and then we did research later on to identify the forms.

After this, we set up the second station. For this, we used water running at high pressure. We had an irrigation pump to get a really high velocity flow. With our irrigation pump, so the water came out the hose fast enough to reach 30 yards away, so it was fast. We aimed the stream at a single spot near the top of a pile and in less than a minute, it had dug halfway through the dirt pile, and had left a huge erosion scar in the side of the pile. The boys took turns using water to dig holes throughout the piles.

We talked at length throughout the day about how effective water is as an agent of change, and while some things that we observe today are obviously made by slow moving water, there are also many things made by fast moving water.

We later researched the many land forms the water made, and made scrapbooks using the photos we took. It was a wonderfully dirty, messy, exciting learning day.

- Sue Moisiadis

The Disappearing Eggshell!

Needed:

egg
vinegar
cup

A simple project we did a couple years ago demonstrated what happens if you don't brush your teeth. We put a raw egg into a cup of vinegar overnight. The shell represented teeth, and the vinegar was, of course, the acid that causes tooth decay. The children were amazed to discover how soft the shell was the next day...fun, and motivation for good hygiene as well!

– Rachel Q

Dancing Raisins !

Needed:

1 can of clear soda (Sprite, 7Up, etc.)

tall glass cup

8 – 10 raisins

Pour the soda into the glass. See the bubbles coming up from the bottom? Those are carbon dioxide gas, which is what is added to soda drinks to give them their fizz.

Drop raisins into the glass and watch them. First they will sink to the bottom of the glass... but then... Watch out! They start dancing!

Why?

The raisins are denser than the soda, so at first they sink to the bottom of the glass. But as the carbon dioxide bubbles form at the bottom of the glass, they cling to the rough serface of the raisins and pull them up to the top along with them. Once they reach the surface and the bubbles pop, the raisins head back down to the bottom again to begin their dance all over!

Try to find some other objects that will "dance" in the soda in a similar manner. Two you can try are uncooked pasta and moth balls. Any others?

Pour Out the Flame!

Needed:

vinegar

baking soda

two cup (or larger) measuring cup

2 or 3 votive candles

What to do:

Do this experiment indoors, in a room with no drafts or moving air.

First, Light your candles.

Next, pour 2-3 ounces of vinegar into your measuring cup, and then add a tablespoon of baking soda. Hold your hand over the measuring cup for a moment as the two bubble and fizz. This chemical reaction is creating carbon dioxide gas. Then, carefully lift the cup and "pour" the invisible gas from the cup over the candle flame. It will go out!

Why? Carbon dioxide is heavier than air, so as you pour it over the candle flame, you are displacing the oxygen needed for the flame to burn. It goes out!

Jumping Flames!

Needed:

Matches

Candle

What to do:

Light a candle, let it burn for a minute, and then blow it out. Quickly hold a burning match to the smoke that is coming from the extinguished wick, and the flame will jump from your match and relight the candle!

Penny Splash !

Needed:
water
pennies
drinking glass

What to do:
Fill the drinking glass completely full of water. Next, one at a time, add pennies to the glass, until water overflows.

How many pennies can you put in a full glass of water? How can you explain this phenomenon? Do you think that other liquids, such as alcohol, would behave in the same way? What did the water look like just before it overflowed?

(The answer can be found in the next experiment!)

Penny Droppers !

Needed:
medicine dropper
penny
dish
water
soap

What to do:
Place the penny flat on the dish. Using the medicine dropper, drip one drop of water at a time onto the surface of the penny. Observe the surface of the water. Try to predict how many drops the surface of the penny will hold before it falls off.

How many drops of water were you able to drip onto the penny before it fell off? What did the water look like just before it fell? Now mix a small amount of soap into your water and try the experiment again. What has changed? Why?

ANSWER: The tendency water has to stick to itself is called "surface tension". You also see this when water bugs walk on water. This is the surface tension of the water holding them up! Adding chemicals such as soap breaks the molecular "hold" of surface tension in water.

ADDITIONAL IDEAS:

Have your kids FIRST guess how many drops of water can be put on top of the coin... they will very likely underestimate it! Try this also with a dime, nickel and quarter!

- scott alan blanchard

Penny Plated Nails !

Needed:
vinegar
salt
small jar with a lid
10 dull pennies
iron nail
steel wool.

What to do:
Place the pennies in the baby food jar. Cover with some
vinegar and 1/2 a teaspoon of salt. Use the steel wool to clean
the pennies. Drop nail into the solution with the pennies and
wait several hours.

What happens? The vinegar
and salt react with the copper
in the penny, causing the
surface molecules to ionize
and float into the vinegar
solution. The iron in the nail
attracts these loose molecules,
which form a thin plating
over the surface of the nail.

Floating Penny Boats !

Needed:
100 pennies
heavy duty aluminum foil
water and large bowl

What to do:
Cut out a 10" square of heavy-duty aluminum foil. Design and fold foil into a boat, using only the foil. Set boat in water and load your boat with pennies (one at a time) until the boat sinks. Record results, redesign your boat, and retest. Try to predict how many pennies each boat model will hold before testing it.

Follow up questions:

What is surface tension?
What is displacement?
Can you come up with a better design for a boat to hold more pennies?

Green Pennies !

Needed:
saucer
paper towel
vinegar
3-5 pennies

What to do:
Fold the paper towel in half; fold again to form a square. Place the folded towel in the saucer. Pour enough vinegar into the saucer to wet the towel. Place the pennies on top of the wet paper towel.

Wait 24 hours. Results: The tops of the pennies are green.

Why? Vinegar's chemical name is acetic acid. The acetate part of the acid combines with the copper on the pennies to form the green coating composed of copper acetate.

Penny in the Well!

Question: How would you get a coin out of a dish of water without touching the water or pouring the water out?

Needed:
dish
matches
jelly jar
water
one candle
penny

What to do:
First fill your dish half way with water. Place a penny in the dish so it is in the water near the edge. Place a jelly jar, with a candle in it, in the center of the dish. Now light the candle. Finally place a jar over the candle. Suddenly the water will rise up in the jar, and the coin will be released.

What happened?

The flame from the candle used up the oxygen in the jelly jar, creating a vacuum which sucks up the water into the jar, exposing the penny.

Penny Halos !

Needed:
50 ml dilute silver nitrate solution
penny
dish

Place silver nitrate solution in dish. Place penny in dish and observe. (you should see a halo of silver wrap around the penny)

Super Clean Pennies!

Question: What cleans pennies better -- an acid or a base solution?

Needed:
1 c water + baking soda
1 c water + Lava soap shavings
1/2 c lemon juice
1 c vinegar
4 cups
20 dirty pennies

What to do:
Baking soda and Lava soap are examples of base solutions.
Lemon juice and vinegar are acid solutions. Which do you
think will clean pennies better? Why? Place five pennies into

each solution. Stir and observe for several minutes. Write whether or not each solution cleaned the dirty penny. Report your findings. Did acids or bases clean the pennies better?

Challenge: Try cleaning other metals in acids and bases. Which metals are the easiest to clean? Which acids or bases make better cleaners?

What's going on: Acids are better penny cleaners. In fact, if you were to leave a penny in vinegar or lemon juice for several days, small pieces of the penny would eventually start to come off. Bases, on the other hand, do not react with metals. Drain cleaners, for example, are bases. Bases do not damage metal pipes like an acid cleaner would.

ADDED IDEA:
Also try using ketchup to clean your pennies! I especially like to do this with nieces/nephews when we would go out to fast food places. I would give them some change and have them put a bit of ketchup on the pennies. Ketchup contains both vinegar and salt, so the chemical reaction that cleans copper happens quickly. Lots of fun!

- Scott Alan Blanchard

The Mystery of the Counterfeit Penny !

Here's a real brain twister... see if you can solve it!

You have eight pennies that look the same, but one is counterfeit. The counterfeit penny is known to be heavier than the others. How can you tell which one is counterfeit by using a balance scale only twice?

Solution: Take two pennies and set them aside. Divide the remaining six pennies into two piles of three each and put them on the balance scale. This is the first use of the balance scale.

If the scale is balanced, then the counterfeit penny must be one of the two pennies that were set aside. Put one on each plate for the second use of the balance scale. The heavier one is the counterfeit.

If the balance scale is not balanced, the counterfeit penny is among the three that weigh more. Take the pile of three pennies that weighs more, and set aside one of them. Then put one penny on each plate (second use of balance scale). If the scale is balanced, the counterfeit penny is the one set aside, otherwise it's the heavier of the two pennies on the scale. This solves the problem using the balance scale only twice.

Penny Powered Cars!

Needed:
two "Matchbox" or "Hot Wheels" cars

ramp (see
instructions)

pennies
tape

What to do:
Set up a ramp for your toy cars (oversized book, cardboard, etc.). Mark a starting line. Let cars run down ramp and across uncarpeted floor. Mark the distance they travel with a piece of tape.

Next, tape a penny to each car and let run down the ramp again. (If you can use little dump trucks to put the pennies that would be best, but taping them to the car is fine.) Mark the distance they travel. Repeat with two pennies each; four pennies each; eight pennies each.

How does the added weight of the pennies affect the distance the cars travel? Why?

The Disappearing Penny !

Needed:
recent (1982 or later) Penny
Cup
Can of Cola

In this experiment, you can either clean another dirty penny...
or make it disappear entirely! And we mean REALLY
disappear!

What to do:
Drop a dirty penny into a cup and pour some Cola or other
carbonated soda into the cup. Look at it again a day later: the
penny has been cleaned! Want to make the penny disappear
completely? Put the penny in a cup of Cola and leave it there
for approximately 10 days. Then pour off the cola (DON'T
drink it), and look: the penny has completely dissolved away!
Now think about your teeth and your stomach when you
drink a soda pop. Hmmmm.... How did it do that?

*The zinc which makes up the body of the penny beneath the copper
jacket is ionized into a zinc 'salt' by the chemicals in the carbonated
soda.*

Old Pennies vs. New Pennies!

In 1982, as a money-saving measure, the U.S. government stopped making pennies out of copper. Since that time, pennies have been made out of zinc, with a thin coat of copper.

What differences are there between the two types of pennies?

On a scale, weigh a stack of ten "old" (pre-1982) pennies and a stack of ten "new" (post 1982) pennies. Which one weighs more? How many new pennies does it take to equal the weight (mass) of ten old pennies? Drop a handful of old pennies on a countertop. Drop a handful of new pennies on a countertop. Is there a difference in the sounds? Which sound do you like better?

Mix up your old and new pennies. Drop them one by one onto the countertop. Try to separate them into "old" and "new" piles by the sound they make only. Then check the dates and see if you got them right.

The Penny Flopover Experiment!

Needed:
10 Pennies
table

What to do:
Set 10 pennies on edge on a table that is not too thick. You will need to be able to lightly tap the underside of the table and cause the pennies to just topple over. The table should be perfectly flat. Pennies should face different directions.

Predict how many of the pennies you think will fall "heads" up and how many you think will fall "tails" up. Write down your prediction.

Next tap the underside of the table gently so that the pennies just topple over. Record the number of heads and tails.

Repeat at least 2 more times. Record your results. Do your results agree with your hypothesis? What do you think would explain these results?

(See next experiment for answers!)

Penny Spinout!

Needed:
10 pennies

What to do:
Take each of the 10 pennies and hold them on edge with your index finger. With your other hand, hit the edge of the penny causing it to spin like a top on the table. When the penny flops over, record whether it is a head or a tail. Do this for all 10 pennies--then repeat at least 2 more times. Again, make a prediction of what you expect the results to be beforehand. Propose a possible explanation for these results.

What happened and why:

The results are that when the pennies fall over (in Experiment 1), they all land heads up! In experiment 2, about 2 out of 3 pennies fall tails up! The reason is that the pennies are actually sections of a cone, not a cylinder, as we assume. The pennies that are placed on their edge actually lean slightly toward the tails side. When disturbed just enough to topple over, they all fall heads up! Very impressive if you use 50 pennies instead of 10! Of course, a few pennies do fall tails--possibly due to dirt or imperfections in the pennies--or to striking the table too hard or using an unlevel table. Spinning the pennies causes the center of gravity to be located toward the tails side. (Think of the penny as spinning on its edge.) This produces the 2/3 tails result when they're spun!

Rocket Powered Pennies !

Needed:
penny
empty glass soda pop bottle
your kitchen freezer

What to do:
Place the empty soda bottle in
the freezer for an hour. Remove
it from the freezer, wet the top
and place a penny over the
mouth of the bottle so it covers it
completely (no air leaks). Now return the bottle to the freezer.

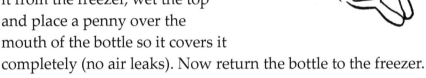

After the bottle has been in the freezer another hour, remove it
and hold it with both hands wrapped around it. Hold tightly
and wait a few minutes and --- POP! What happened??????

Solution:
*Heat causes objects to expand (get bigger), while cold causes objects
to contract (get smaller). This includes air, and it includes the air
INSIDE the frozen pop bottle. When you place your warm hands
around the outside of the bottle, it warms the air inside the bottle
which then expands. Since the bottle is sealed by the penny, the
heated air can only escape by breaking the ice around the rim and
forcing the penny out of the way. When the build up of heated air
inside the bottle grows great enough, the ice gives and -- POW! the
penny pops off the bottle!*

Penny Mushroom Pile!

Needed:
thread spool
lots of pennies!

What to do:
Challenge your patience and dexterity! Try piling pennies on a spool of thread. The catch however, is to pile outward, not up, forming a large mushroom. See how wide a "mushroom head" you can form and challenge your siblings or parents to do better!

Electric Salt & Pepper!

Needed:

Salt and Pepper

zip lock sandwich bag

paper plate, balloon

What to do: While teaching a class of about 8 children about electricity, I did a demonstration that got a big wow. I took salt, and mixed it with pepper in a zip lock bag. I asked the students if they would be able to separate the salt from the pepper, and how long did they think it would take to do it? After each examining the bag, they concluded that it would take too long, and maybe even be impossible.

I told them that I could do it in a matter of seconds using the power of electricity.

I poured the salt and pepper mixture onto a paper plate. I blew up a balloon, and rubbed the balloon on a volunteer's head until static was generated. (A sweater or wool jacket would also work, but it's not as personal.) I then placed the balloon about an inch above the mixture, and presto! The pepper rose up and clung to the balloon. They were amazed, and immediately wanted to try it themselves. They each got a turn, and couldn't wait to get home to show their families. I took a moment to explain that the static electricity was able to lift the pepper because it is lighter than the salt, and that electricity is all around us. Simple, elegant, and hair raising!

- Karen Steele

Ice on a String !

Needed:
bowl of water
several ice cubes
a string
salt

(Optional) to prove that most other materials don't do the same thing, use other substances such as pepper, dirt, dried herbs, baking soda, and sugar.

This experiment demonstrates the ability of salt to lower the freezing point of water. You can tailor the amount of information provided to suit the level of the child. My 7 year old was fascinated by this and had fun coming up with other substances to try. An older child can use this to learn more about chemistry and how different substances affect each other.

What to do:
1. Drop the ice into the water.
2. Place the string onto the ice cube.
3. Sprinkle some salt on it.
4. WAIT for at least 15 to 20 seconds.
5. Pick up the ice cube and be amazed!
6. (Optional) Repeat the steps for each additional substance and take note of which ones worked or didn't work.

Explanation:

Salt dissolved in water lowers the freezing point. This causes the water on the ice to melt and allows the string to sink slightly into the ice cube. After a few seconds the ice refreezes around the string, trapping it in the cube.

This happens with any dissolved substance (the sugar and baking soda should work the same way that salt does) because the dissolved particles (ions) interfere with the hydrogen bonds between the water molecules that give the ice its structure. These substances also cause the water to boil at a higher temperature, which is why we add salt to cooking water!

- Kim Dickey

Ice Cream in a Bag !

Combine:

2 Tbs. of sugar

1 cup of Half and Half

½ tsp. vanilla extract

in a ziplock bag and seal tight.

Place ½ cup salt (pickling salt or rock salt works best) in a gallon size bag, then fill it halfway with ice cubes. Place the sealed smaller bag inside the ice bag , seal and start the reaction. Roll or shake the bag for about 5 min. Feel the small bag to determine when its done... and eat the ice cream right out of the bag if you want. Yum!

Science notes:

By constantly disturbing the ice crystals, you end up with lots of small crystals instead of a few larger ones. This makes the texture of the ice cream smooth.

The mixing also traps air bubbles in the mix, making it fluffy and lighter. As a separate experiment, you can see how much air they mix with store bought ice cream by letting some melt and then refreeze. You will find that it shrinks by almost 1/3 of its size once the air bubbles come out.

if you want to be a dedicated scientist, you could also test to see whether adding chocolate syrup to the mixture changes the way that it freezes. Of course, you should also test it with fresh strawberries , blueberries, peaches…)

- Jennifer Koontz

Forensic DNA Identification!

Needed:

Cut out 8-10 UPC bar codes from various products.

Put them on the xerox machine and make a copy of all of them.

Take that copy and use a sharpie marker to mark up and degrade the bar codes (so it isn't too easy).

What to do:

Pick one of your originals to become the "suspect".

On the degraded copy add the unmarked UPC suspect, label all the degraded samples with a letter and make a new copy.

Now you have 8-10 degraded samples and a clean original on the same paper.

Make enough copies for your students and ask them to match the suspect code to the rest.

Finally they announce (or record) who they accuse of the crime. Keep them mindful that if they accuse the wrong person they send an innocent person to jail.

- Bruce Boehne

All Mixed Up 1: Crazy Writing !

Needed:
Pencil
paper

What to do:
Sit down at a table, and pick
up a pencil and write your
name on a piece of paper.
Easy, huh?

Now make your foot go in a circle as you are sitting, and try to
write your name again. You'll find you can barely do it, if at all
-- your name will be a crazy looking scrawl on the paper! If
you are able to do it, then try again while making your foot
go in a circle the opposite way. Tough, isn't it?

Why?

Your brain can't control both the movement of your leg and
your hand at the same time, and will tend to transfer the
movement of your leg to your hand. Similarly, your
concentration is broken when studying while listening to
music, or watching TV, etc.

All Mixed Up 2: Backwards Foot!

What to do:

Sit down and cross your legs, with the right leg on top. Rotate your right foot clockwise. Now, while you are doing that, use your right finger to "draw" a number "6" in the air. You'll find that this makes you reverse the direction of your foot, so it is now rotating anti-clockwise!

All Mixed Up 3: Hit the Dot!

Needed:
pencil
paper

What to do:

Using a pencil, put a dot on a piece of paper and set it on the table in front of you. Next, hold the pencil up to your shoulder, then bring it down right on the dot. Easy peasy!

Now, close one eye and try again to bring the pencil down right on the dot. NOT so easy, is it? Try again with the other eye closed. Hard!

Why?

We are used to seeing with binocular vision - that is, seeing objects using both eyes. Each eye sees something from a slightly different angle, and this enables our brain to accurately to perceive depth, distance and location. When we use just one eye, it throws off our ability to perceive the exact location of the dot on the paper, and so makes it very hard to hit it the first time out!

All Mixed Up 4: Mirror Writing!

Needed:
Index card
pencil

What to do:
Hold the index card right up to your forehead, and write your name on it. Then take a look at the card. You wrote your name backwards! By habit, you wrote from left to right, like you normally write.

Ice Tunnels !

Needed:

Some plastic tubs or containers (you can use food packages such as cottage cheese tubs, etc.)

Water

Salt

Freezer

What to do:

Freeze ice in different sized containers. The next day dump the blocks of ice out of their containers and set them on a cookie tray with a lip. Then dump salt in a bowl and then mix it with liquid watercolor. pour that on our blocks of ice and let them sit in the sun for a few minutes and watch the changes that take place.

We explain to our kids that the salt lowers the freezing point of water and the salt makes "tunnels" in the ice as it corrodes the walls of the ice block. We give them the primary colors in liquid water color and let them explore the different colors they can make. This is something they can come back to hours later and see the changes that have occurred. Most fascinating for early elementary.

Soda Can Implosion !

Needed:
Clean pop can
tongs
large bowl of ice water
stove

Directions:

Have the large bowl of ice water close by and ready to go.

Add a generous tablespoon of water to the pop can.

Set the can directly on a stovetop burner, waiting until you can see water vapor coming out of the hole in the top of the can.

Quickly invert (flip over) the can into the bowl of water.

The can will "POP" (loudly!) and implode.

Repeat . . . again, and again, and again.

- Heather Wiegand

Elephant Toothpaste!

Needed:

hydrogen peroxide

food coloring

dish detergent

1 tsp. Dry yeast

empty plastic soda bottle

cookie sheet

water

This is something we call "elephant toothpaste". We call it this because it resembles toothpaste being squeezed from a tube, and there is a LOT of it!

What to do:

Put a 16 ounce plastic bottle on a cookie sheet. This is to catch the "overflow". You will not want to forget this...

Mix 1/2 cup hydrogen peroxide and a few drops food coloring. it is easiest to use a funnel to add these to the bottle, but not necessary. Add a squirt of dish detergent. in a separate bowl, mix 1 teaspoon of yeast and dissolve it in 2 tablespoons of warm water. Add this to the bottle. if using a funnel be sure to remove it right away as this experiment reacts rather quickly. When mixed, the foam will come flowing out of the bottle looking very much like toothpaste coming out a tube!

Super fun to make and safe to touch!

What is Happening?

This foam is special because each tiny bubble is filled with oxygen! The yeast acted as a catalyst (a helper) to remove the oxygen from the hydrogen peroxide (that's right, peroxide means oxygen!). Since this reaction was very fast, the separation created Lots of bubbly foam. It also created something else cool – an Exothermic Reaction! This means not only was foam made, so was heat! The next time you do the experiment, feel the bottle while adding the yeast-water. The bottle will warm up!

  – Kimmie Olson with additions by Mrs. Sims

Balloon Blow Pop Bottle!

Needed:

Empty 8 oz water bottle
2 tbs. baking soda
Balloon
Vinegar

What to do:

Put baking soda in a
balloon

Fill your bottle 2/3 to half way with vinegar (white works
good)

Carefully fit the top of the balloon onto the rim of the bottle

Without letting any baking soda fall out (keep it bent in half)

Once the balloon is secure, lift the balloon part with the
baking soda in it and let the baking soda empty into the
bottle... and _wow_ the balloon blows up!

The more baking soda and vinegar you have the more it will
blow up!

- the Schaefer family

Homemade Vinegar Grenades!

Needed:
vinegar
baking soda
ziplock snack or sandwich bag

What to do:
We measured 1/2 cup vinegar and set it aside. Then we put 1/4 cup baking soda into a ziplock baggie twisting it into one corner. We poured in the vinegar and squished as much air out as possible before sealing while keeping the baking soda twisted. Once the bag was well sealed we untwisted the baking soda corner, shook the bag and threw it out in our alley.

As the vinegar and baking soda mixed and began reacting, the resulting gas inflated the baggie and eventually blew the baggie up.

We explain that the sodium bicarbonate as baking soda and the acid in vinegar form carbonic acid which degrades immediately to carbon dioxide, the gas that fills the baggie and bursts it. Then we clean up the baggie!!!

– Jennifer Hartnagle

Soap Power!

Needed:

styrofoam tray (from grocery meat, etc.)

dishwashing liquid

tub with water in it

What to do:

Cut two identical boat (or house) shaped pentagons from styrofoam trays - four to five inches long. Fill a tub with a few inches of water. Place a spot of dish soap at the back of one boat on the bottom. Place both boats in the water at one end of the tub. Watch them go!

The one without soap should just follow the movement of the water, while the one with soap should scoot along. This demonstrates how soap breaks the surface tension of the water, and in this case, propels the "boat" forward.

- Heather Matson

Water Tension Magic!

Needed:

black pepper

bowl

watercolor

dishwashing liquid

What to do:
We fill a bowl with water and gently sprinkle the surface with black pepper. We explain that the black pepper floats because of water tension, where the water molecules are conjoined in such a way they form a semi-solid surface, the same thing that allows them to form drops or to bulge over the edge of a very full glass without spilling. We even put a finger in and watch the pepper "run away" because we are shoving the water over, like bunching a blanket.

Then we put one drop of dish soap in the center of the water and the pepper all falls to the bottom. Soap breaks the bond, destroying water tension, which is why it gets our dishes, clothes and hands clean. Without soap, water sticks only to water and leaves dirt alone, but when we break up the molecules they can slip past the dirt and get it off.

- Jennifer Hartnagle

Gel Bead Fun !

Needed:

Florist water gel beads

This activity has to do with <u>teaching Scientific inquiry</u>. it all started when my 13-year-old daughter bought a pouch of florist's water gel beads at the craft store. One small pouch of dry gel beads costing ~$2.50. this pouch makes several quarts of gel "marbles" when reconstituted.

There are so many hypotheses that can be made and tested using these gel beads! The results are available in about 6 hours, so kids can complete a full experiment in one day's time. One packet makes so many beads, it should allow kids to perform any number of experiments and to repeat experiments if they want to try to duplicate their results.

Kids can practice developing a hypothesis, limiting variables, conducting the experiment (without handling hazardous tools or chemicals--just **don't eat** the beads!!!), and observing and reporting the results. They might explore predictions about:

--how water temperature affects rehydration time
--how room temperature or humidity affect rehydration time
--how different liquids might affect the rehydrated beads (size, color, volume)
--how the different liquids themselves might be affected when used to rehydrate the gel beads
--how the rehydrated beads might change when frozen, heated, dried, etc.

Math skills can include weighing (a gram scale works best), measuring and comparing volume, charting hour-by-hour changes and calculating ratios and percents for older students.

Language skills can include expository writing and using accurate, descriptive language.

Art skills can include photography, sketching and designing a poster. The gel beads left from your experiments make a beautiful addition to clear glass vases so the kids can even try their hand at flower arranging!

These gel beads are fun to play with when you are done too...they bounce like crazy! in fact, we recommend taking measurements over a cookie sheet with a lip to help contain run-away beads.

- Rose-Marie Gallagher

Homemade Lava Lamp!

Needed:
Empty soda Bottle
Vegetable Oil
Water
Alka-Seltzer
Food Coloring

What to do:
1. Fill bottle 2/3 full of oil.
2. Finish filling with water. The water will sink to the bottom.
3. Add food coloring. it is water based and will go through the oil and mix with the water below.
4. Break an Alka-Seltzer tablet into small pieces and drop them one at a time into the bottle.
5. Watch your lava lamp erupt. As it slows down, add more Alka-Seltzer.
Note: Don't add too much Alka-Seltzer or the liquid will over flow the bottle.

Why it works: A cup of water has more mass than a cup of oil. When putting the two liquids together, the water will sink to the bottom of the container because water is more dense than oil.

- Mandy Blackmon

Black Magic !

We ended up doing this experiment inadvertently when we did our Lava Lamp. My son added so many different colors that his water turned black. After adding too much Alka-Seltzer and exploding his lava lamp all over the counter we had a quick cleanup in progress and viola we had tie-dyed paper towels. It was really great, but then I needed to look up the why?

Needed:
Paper coffee filter
Black water color marker
Scissors
Water
Cup

What to do:

First cut the center circle out of the coffee filter, so you have a paper "ring". Next with a black marker, draw a line about an inch from the bottom across the circle. Put enough water in the cup to cover the bottom. Curl the paper to fit inside the cup making sure the bottom of the circle is in the water. Watch as the water moves up the filter, when it touches the black line you will start seeing different colors. Leave the paper in the water until the colors have reached the edge. How many different colors do you see? Try repeating this with different water color markers and see if you get different results.

Why is this Happening?

Most water color markers are made of different color pigments and water. On a coffee filter, the water spreads the pigment onto the paper and when it dries the pigment stays. Different colored pigments are carried along at different rates, some moving faster than others.

- Mandy Blackmon

Clattering Peas !

Needed:
Bag of dried peas
Wine glass or goblet
metal pie pan
water

What to do:
Place your wine glass on the metal pie pan, then fill it to overflowing with the dried peas. Carefully pour water into the peas, up to the brim of the glass.

Over the next few minutes/hours, the heap of peas will slowly absorb the water. (This is the osmotic process - the cells in the peas absorb the moisture, stretching and expanding as they do so.) As they do, the peas will tap-tap-tap one at a time onto the pie pan, as they fall out of the glass. This clatter will go on for hours!

Multi-Colored Flowers!

Needed:
two small drinking glasses
two colors of food coloring (red and blue, for instance)
a white flower, such as a carnation or rose
sharp knife or razor blade
water

What to do:
Fill the two small drinking glasses half full of water. Put several drops of food coloring in each glass. Put one color in one glass, and the second color in the other glass. Now carefully split the stem of your flower with the knife, being careful not to cut yourself or the counter top. (Put some newspapers or

cardboard under the stem if needed.) Put the glasses side by side, and put one part of the stem in one glass, and the second part of the stem in the second glass. Over the next few hours, your flower will turn colors: half red and half blue!

Why? All plants and flowers need moisture, and draw it up from the ground through their roots and stems. The colored liquid flows up through the stem into the flower itself. The veins of the flower turn their respective colors due to the side of the stem they draw their moisture from.

Humming Glasses !

Needed:

some thin-walled goblets or wine glasses
water

What to do:
First, wash your hands thoroughly with soap
and water. Next, fill the glass about half full
with water. Dip your index finger in the water,
then very slowly run your finger around the
rim of the glass. You'll soon hear a continuous
humming tone from the glass.

Put different amounts of water into your
remaining glasses, and try the same with
them. The amount of water in each glass
affects the pitch of the tone you will get from each glass.

If your finger is dirty or greasy, this won't work. As your clean
finger rubs along the rim of the glass, it ever so slightly creates
some friction, vibrating the glass and produces the tones you
hear. You can also see the water in the glass vibrating if you
watch it carefully.

See if you can make different notes with your glasses, and
even play a simple song. Just be careful not to spill the water
or break your glasses.

Burning Sugar !

Needed:
Cube of sugar
pie pan
match or lighter
some ashes

What to do:
Place some ashes (from a fireplace, or a cigarette, etc.) on the pie pan and try to light them. They won't burn.

Next, place your sugar cube on the pie pan (don't touch the ashes!) and try to light it with your match or lighter. It won't burn either.

Now, dip the corner of the sugar cube in the ashes and try to light it again from that corner. This time, the cube will burn (with a pretty blue flame) until it is completely burned up.

Why? Neither the ashes nor the sugar cube will burn on their own, but when mixed together, they ignite. The ash makes the sugar cube combustible. The ash, in this case, is a "catalyst" that causes a chemical reaction in the sugar.

Incredi-Bubble Experiments !

Okay, first things first....

Here is the formula you will need to create the "incredi-bubble" solution, which will give you longer-lasting, extra big, extra fun bubbles. This is, bar-none, the best solution for making bubbles...the same recipe that is used in museum exhibits across the country.

Here it is:
1 Cup liquid detergent - Liquid Joy works well.
10 Cups water
And the secret ingredient for extra strong bubbles --
4 tablespoons Glycerine (Available at drugstores.) That's all!

Just stir it together gently, so suds don't form.

HINT: If you allow it to sit uncovered in a bowl for 24 hours, it will be produce much stronger, longer lasting bubbles.
Have fun!

Bubble Wands

Those little plastic bubble wands that come with bottles of store-bought bubble solution work fine, but you don't have to limit yourself only to those. Bubble wands can be created out of all sorts of objects: straws, pipe cleaners, strawberry baskets, loops of wire, rope or string, etc.

A coat hanger makes an especially good, BIG bubble wand: bend it into a circular shape, then wrap the metal with string or strips of rags. This will hold lots of bubble solution and will make truly huge bubbles.

Giant Man-Eating Bubbles

Materials needed:

hula hoop string or cloth pipe clamp
3' of pvc pipe
bubble solution (a LOT of it!)
small kiddie wading pool
plastic milk crate

What to do:
Attach the piece of PVC pipe to the hula hoop using the pipe clamp. This will give you a "handle" to hold the hoop by during this experiment. Wrap string or cloths around the hula hoop so it will "hold onto" the bubble solution longer.

You'll want two or more students to participate in this experiment. Have the student stand on the crate in the middle of the wading pool. Fill the wading pool about 1/4 full of bubble solution. Place the bubble wand into the solution and quickly bring it up over the student. A second student can measure the width of the bubble. A third student can time the duration of each bubble. Kids love this activity, so be sure to make plenty of time for it!

HINTS:

1. Keep the ruler wet when measuring bubbles. 2. Use a vinegar and water solution in a spray bottle to clean up. 3. Use goggles when enclosing students in the giant bubbles. 4. Have observers stay away from the wading pool because the area becomes very slippery. 5. This is a good unit to introduce quantitative and qualitative observation.

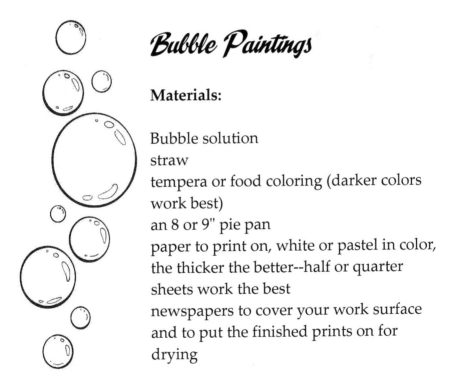

Bubble Paintings

Materials:

Bubble solution
straw
tempera or food coloring (darker colors work best)
an 8 or 9" pie pan
paper to print on, white or pastel in color, the thicker the better--half or quarter sheets work the best
newspapers to cover your work surface and to put the finished prints on for drying

What to do:
1. Lay out the newspapers to cover your work area. 2. Pour

bubble solution in pan approximately 1/4" deep. 3. Stir in thoroughly 1-2 teaspoons paint. 4. Stick the end of the straw into the liquid and blow very gently to make bubbles covering the surface of the liquid. 5. Holding a piece of paper by the edges, lay it down on the surface of the bubbles. Press down slightly to pop some of the bubbles, but don't let go of the paper or let it touch the liquid. 6. Lay the paper face up to dry. if you don't like how it turned out, you can print the paper over again one or more times, or even use a different color of paint. 7. After paper has dried, flatten under some heavy books before using it.

Ideas:

What do the bubble prints look like without adding any coloring? What other things can you blow bubbles with? Try using more than one color in your print. How can you print one big bubble?

Ponder those bubbles for a few moments...

How many of these questions about bubbles can YOU answer?

1. Bubbles last longer on humid days (like right after it has rained) than on dry days. Why?
2. What could you use to make lots of tiny bubbles?
3. How could you measure a bubble? (Hint: use a ruler covered with bubble solution).

4. Why do bubbles fall towards the ground?
5. Try catching a bubble with a dry hand and then try again with a wet hand. Which lasts longer? Why?
6. Why are bubbles round?
7. What happens when two bubbles meet each other?
8. Can you blow a lasting bubble with pure water?
9. Where do bubbles' colors come from?

Answers:

1. The moisture in the bubble doesn't evaporate as fast. 2. Start experimenting and find out! 3. Try a ruler covered with bubble solution. 4. The weight of the water and bubble solution is heavier than air. 5. Wet hands are better, because the surface tension of the bubble is less likely to be broken or dried out. 6. When you blow a bubble, the tension in the bubble skin tries to shrink the bubble into a shape with the smallest possible surface area for the volume of air it contains. That shape happens to be a sphere. 7. The bubbles will merge together and share a common surface, or wall. if both bubbles are the same size, the wall will be flat. if they are different sizes, the smaller bubble will bulge into the larger bubble, which has a lower internal pressure. 8. No. The surface tension of pure water is too strong to allow bubbles to form. Soapy solutions reduce the surface tension of water, allowing it to stretch much easier. The soap also prevents the water from evaporating quickly, which prolongs the life of a bubble greatly. 9. Light waves are bent by the liquid and convex surface of the bubble.

Incredible Crystal Experiments !

The Magic Salt Crystal Garden

Materials:
Something hard but porous: a piece of brick, lump of charcoal, charcoal briquets, or piece of cement. (Charcoal briquets are best if they are not the quick -start type, with added chemicals.)
Table salt; 2 Tbsp.
Water; 2 Tbsp.
Laundry bluing; 2 Tbsp.
Household ammonia; 2 Tbsp.

What to do:
Put the charcoal briquets into a shallow dish or pie pan.
Mix the four chemicals.
Pour the mixture over the cement.
Add a couple drops of food coloring onto briquets if desired.
Crystals will begin forming in just a few hours, and will continue to grow over several days.
Don't touch or bump, as crystals are very fragile.
If you wish to, you may add the same amount of the chemicals every few days to keep crystals growing. Pour gently into dish (not on top of crystals).

Why do crystals form?

As the water in your solutions evaporates, the molecules of solid substances in the liquid (solute) link back together in patterns that reflect the shape of the molecules. (For instance, salt crystals are cube-shaped, because salt molecules are cube-shaped; sugar crystals are oblong and flat, because sugar molecules are oblong and flat; bluing crystals are feathery, etc.) Solid materials in which the molecules are arranged in repeating patterns like this are **crystals***.*

Cool Cave Stalagtites

Needed:
washing soda (get at grocery)
hot tap water
foot-long piece of string
2 baby food jars
two washers
small dish

Tie a washer to each end of the string. Fill the two jars with hot water and stir in washing soda until no more will dissolve in the water. Place the ends of your string into the two jars, with the ends of the string touching the bottom of the jars. Put the dish between the two jars so you have a loose, drooping string "bridge" hanging over it, from one jar to the other. Let sit for 4 or 5 days. A cave-like stalagtite (formation that grows down from the ceiling) and stalagmite (formation that grows up from the floor) will start to grow over the dish at its lowest point.

Creeping Crystals

Needed:

1 T epsom salt
1 T water
1/4 t food color (any but yellow)
2 2" jar lids
spoon

Pour epsom salt & water into saucepan. Stir & cook over medium heat until salt dissolves. Remove from heat and stir in food coloring. Pour into first jar lid until almost full. Pour any extra into second lid. As liquid evaporates, crystals will start to form. Over several days, they will grow up and over the lid. They will last for months.

Creeping Crystal Paint

Make the Creeping Crystal formula given previously. Add an extra 1/4 t of food color to the mix. Brush onto paper, cardboard or glass -- as it dries, frost-like, feathery crystals will appear on the painted surface.

Salt Crystal Cubes

Needed:

1/2 cup table salt
1 cup water glass
cotton string
paper clip
pencil

Mix salt and water until salt is dissolved. Pour into drinking glass. Tie a paper clip to one end of a short piece of string and tie the other end around a pencil. Lay the pencil across the top of the glass and suspend the string and paper clip in the salt water solution. Put in a place (a sunny window is best) where it will not be shaken or disturbed and observe for two or three weeks. As the water evaporates, salt rock crystals will form on the string and paper clip. The longer you wait, the bigger the crystals will get. The salt crystals will be cube shaped, which reflects the molecular structure of salt.

(For colored crystals, add a few drops of food coloring when first mixing your salt solution.)

Incredible Mouth Experiments!

Map Your Tongue

The four basic tastes we taste are: salt, sweet, bitter, and sour. But did you know that only a certain area of your tongue can taste each of these tastes? in this experiment, you will make a map of your tongue and locate the specific areas where the four basic tastes can be tasted.

Materials:
Cotton Swabs Twisted to a Point
tiny amounts of: Salt, Sugar, Pure Lemon Juice, Tonic Water or

Black Coffee
4 Small Dixie Cups
Four Different Colored Pencils
Distilled Water
Spoons
Copy of tongue map on following page

What to do:
Prepare weak solutions of the four basic tastes. Fill the four dixie cups with distilled water. Stir a small amount of sugar into one of the containers until it can be slightly but definitely tasted. Repeat procedure for the salt, lemon juice, and coffee . Dip the pointed end of the cotton swab into the salt solution and then gently dab a tiny amount to a spot on your tongue. if you taste salt in the solution, mark the spot with a small colored X (a different color should be used for each solution) on the Tongue Map. if you do not taste salt in the solution, do not mark that spot. Continue until the entire tongue is tested. (Be careful when you dab close to the back of the tongue. You might gag yourself!)

When you have tested the whole surface of your tongue with one solution, rinse with distilled water and repeat with each of the remaining solutions.

Once you have completed the testing, you will have several small colored "x's" on your tongue map. The "x's" should show very specific areas of your tongue that are sensitive to sweet, salt, sour and bitter. Draw a circle around each section to differentiate the areas of taste.

My Tongue Map

Showing where I taste sweet, salt, sour & bitter

Back of tongue

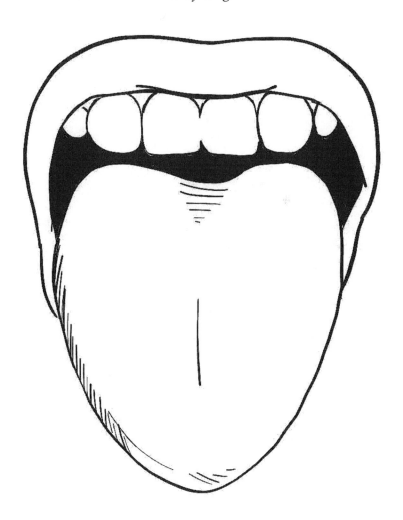

Front of tongue

Rock Breath

Materials:

Powdered Lime (not the fruit, but the pickling chemical available at your grocery)
a straw
2 pint jars

What to do:

Fill jar with water. Add one tablespoon of lime and stir. Screw on the lid and let the solution stand for 12 or more hours. Pour off half of the clear liquid into the second jar very carefully. Don't let any of the settled lime sneak in.

Use the straw to exhale your breath slowly into the limewater, until the clear limewater turns a milky color.

Why does this happen -- and what is that stuff in the jar?

Limewater always turns milky when carbon dioxide (CO_2) is mixed with it. The chemical in the limewater is dissolved calcium oxide (CaO). This combines with the CO_2 gas to form a white powder that will not dissolve in water. This white powder is actually limestone! Limestone is calcium carbonate ($CaCO_3$). if the solution is able to stand for several hours, the powdery limestone should settle to the bottom of the jar.

Stuffy Smellers

Materials:
Blindfold
Swimmer's Nose Plug (or you can hold nose with fingers)
Small peeled cubes of potato, apple, and onion

What to do:
Put on a blindfold and plug your nose. Have another person put one of the cubes into your mouth. Try to guess what food it is. Repeat with the other samples.

What effect does your sense of smell have on your sense of taste?

Tasting Hot and Cold

Materials:
orange juice

What to do:
Pour some orange juice in an ice tray and let freeze. Pour some more in a cup and heat in microwave until very warm (not burning hot). Hold the frozen orange juice cube in your mouth for fifteen seconds. How strong is the taste? Next, take a drink of the warm juice and hold in your mouth for fifteen seconds. What effect does temperature have on your sense of taste?

HERE ARE A FEW MORE
TASTY SCIENCE FACTS FOR YOU:

* The number of taste buds in our mouths changes throughout your life. Babies and children have many more taste buds than adults and adults lose more and more taste buds as they grow older. That's why many older people often eat less, and like spicier foods than kids.

* Insects like house flies and butterflies have taste buds on their feet. How would a meal be in your house if everyone's taste buds were on their feet?

* Taste buds have a life span of less than ten days. They are then replaced by new ones.

Disappearing Gum

Can you make a portion of a stick of gum disappear (without swallowing it)? This experiment will show you how this happens every time you chew a stick of gum -- and just what it is that disappears!

Materials:
2 sticks of chewing gum or bubble gum
small kitchen or postage scale

What to do:
Remove the wrapper from your gum. Weigh it on your scale and record. Put it in your mouth and chew it for ten minutes, until the flavor is about gone. Take out gum and let dry for 24 hours. Now weigh the wad of gum.

You should find that it weighs only about 2/3 of its original weight. Take your second piece of gum and tear off a portion of that piece until it weighs the same as your chewed gum wad. This will show you just how much mass the gum has lost.

Can you guess what part of the gum disappeared when you chewed it? Your gum lost the sugar that was mixed in the gum to sweeten it. Just think -- a piece of gum is over 1/3 sugar! Makes it easy to see where cavities come from, doesn't it?

Fireworks in Your Mouth

Did you know that crushing certain flavored Life Savers candies in your mouth can set off sparks? This experiment will demonstrate how light can be given off by a simple chemical reaction.

Materials:
A roll of "Wint-O-Green" mint Life Savers
a very dark room
a hand mirror or partner

What to do:
Give your eyes a few minutes to adjust to the dark room before starting experiment. With a partner (or looking in the mirror) in a dark room, crunch the mint with your teeth with your mouth open. Your partner should see sparks of light generated when you bite on the candy.

Reverse the roles so that you can see the sparks in your partner's mouth. You can also achieve the same results by hitting the Life Savers with a hammer on a hard surface to observe the same quality of sparks.

Why does it do this?

When the candy is crushed, the friction of unlike charges (positive and negative, or + and -) causes loose particles called electrons to start a series of interactions between the nitrogen in the air, sugar, and candy molecules. This type of light is called "triboluminescence".

Awful Orange Juice

Needed:
toothbrush
toothpaste
orange juice

What to do:
Take a sip of orange juice and note the different strengths of sweet, bitter and sour flavor on different parts of your tongue. Rinse your mouth out with water.

Next, brush your teeth briskly for one minute. Rinse your mouth. Now take a sip of orange juice again. For about 1/3 of people, the orange juice will still taste the same. But for 2/3 of people, it will taste very bitter.

Why?
About 2/3 of us have a "taste gene" on our tongue that greatly enhances our ability to detect bitter tastes. 1/3 of us do not have this gene. Almost all toothpastes contain an ingredient called sodium lauryl sulfate (SLS). SLS causes sweet tastes (sugar) to decrease, and at the same time causes bitter tastes to be strengthened almost ten times their original intensity. The sour/bitter taste of orange juice comes from citric acid. After brushing your teeth, you are tasting 10 times the amount of citric acid as normal! Yuck!

Ocean In A Bottle!

An "Ocean in a Bottle" is not only a neat toy -- it is a fascinating and fun way to study how water moves and waves work. it is a relatively easy to make one, as well.

Needed:
One clear, plastic bottle with a twist-on cap (20 oz. or larger soft drink bottles are just right. A 2 or 3 liter bottle can be even more fun, though it is **quite** heavy.

Rubbing alcohol (water may be substituted for rubbing alcohol, but it produces too many bubbles when the bottle is shaken, and is not recommended)

Blue/green food coloring

Mineral Spirits or Turpentine (Mineral Spirits is much cheaper) *

glue or duct tape

What to do:
Step 1: Fill your bottle 1/2 full of rubbing alcohol. Add several drops of food coloring. Shake to mix.

Step 2: Fill the bottle the rest of the way full with Mineral Spirits. Leave as little space for air bubbles as possible.

Step 3: Secure the bottle cap so it will not come off. You can do this by either applying glue to the threads of the cap, then screwing it on, or you can wrap the cap tightly with duck tape.

Your "Ocean in a Bottle" is now complete! Tip it, turn it, swirl it, shake it, explore and have fun!

Questions to ponder:

As you experiment with and examine your "Ocean in a Bottle", try to figure out the answers to the following questions. (Answers are in the following sections.)

1. How are waves generated?

2. What is the source of this energy?

3. What are some of the causes of waves?

4. How are the most important types of ocean waves generated?

5. What are some other things needed for a wave?

6. What is the recipe for a wave? (answer at the end of this section)

7. Describe the action of a wave. Does a wave make the water move along with it, or does a wave move through the water?

8. How can waves be changed?

9. If something happens inside the bottle, does it affect all the water? Would the motion of waves could carry and disperse pollution?

Some Definitions:

A "wave" is a moving disturbance on or through water, which does not move the water itself.

Wind causes waves by frictional drag. Waves not pushed by strong winds are called "swells".

Waves "break" as they near shore when they "feel bottom", a depth shallower than 1/2 the wave's length.

Away from shore, when the depth of the water is at least 1 1/3 times the height of a wave, the wave front is so steep the top falls over and the wave "breaks".

The wave activity between the line of breakers and the shore is called the "surf".

As the water moves up the beach, it loses its energy and flows back into the water --this backward flow is called "backwash".

How Waves Work

Water in oceans and lakes is in constant motion. it moves by wind-generated waves, tides, tsunamis (seismic waves), and a variety of density currents.

All waves are a means of moving some form of energy from one place to another. All waves must be generated by some source of energy. The most important types of ocean waves are generated by wind.

As wind moves over the open ocean, the turbulent air distorts the surface where they move downward, and as they move upward, they cause a decrease in pressure which elevates the water surface. These changes in pressure produce an irregular, wavy surface in the ocean and transfer part of the wind's energy into water. in a stormy sea, waves tend to be choppy and irregular. As waves move out from their place of origin, the shorter waves move more slowly and are left behind, and the patterns develop some measure of order.

As a wave approaches the shore, it collapses forward, or breaks, into a surf. The water then rushes forward to the shore and returns to backwash.

Wave motion can easily be observed by watching a floating object move forward as the crest of a wave approaches and then sinks back into the following trough. You can move your "ocean in a jar" to duplicate this movement.

The motion of water in waves is distinctly different from the motion in currents. in currents, the water moves in a given direction and does not return to its original position.

The energy of a wave depends on its length and height. Students should have a model to observe of wave and trough during a discussion of wavelength, height and crest.

Answer to Recipe for a Wave:
a. form of energy; b. water; c. surface

Incredible Guck Experiments!

Toys such as *Gak!*, *Silly Putty*, *Floam*, *Smud*, and our homemade GUCK recipe are made up of polymerized chemicals. Polymers basically consist of long "chains" of molecules that are flexible and that cross-link (or tangle up) every which way. When the right chemicals are mixed together, the molecules from the chemicals cross-link together and create a polymerized "liquid".

For instance, when you mix plain old Elmer's glue (which contains latex) with sodium borate (Borax), a chemical reaction occurs: The Borax causes the latex molecules in the glue to cross-link together (or "polymerize") in long chains. These chains link to other chains nearby, and as a result, you have what we call GUCK!

Polymers have truly interesting qualities. Though they are liquids, they don't flow like other liquids. instead, they can ooze, cling to things and even climb walls. This is because they have a much higher viscosity (thickness, or resistance to flowing) than ordinary fluids.

If you pull a polymer like GUCK slowly, the molecules are able to hold together, and it stretches out in thin strands (those are the chain-linked molecules mentioned above). if you pull it quickly or whack it with a hammer, the molecules can't hold together, and it snaps or shatters. Put two pieces of GUCK together, and the molecules in the two pieces will quickly begin to link back together. interesting, huh? So let's makes some!

How to Make Guck

Mix together:
1 cup white glue (like Elmer's) and 1-1/2 cup water.
Add food coloring or tempera paint to desired color.

In a separate bowl:
Mix 1-1/2 Tablespoons Borax and 1/2 cup water. (Borax can be found in the laundry-detergent section of the grocery store under the brand name "20 Mule Team Borax") Stir until the powder dissolves.

Now, pour borax solution into the bowl containing the glue. Keep stirring it as you pour, or the borax will settle.

Instantly, a chemical reaction will take place, and a thick glob will form in the bowl. Take out your stirring spoon and roll up your sleeves. Squish and knead the mixture with your hands (the kids love this part) until all the liquid in the bowl is absorbed into the glob. Voila! You've made guck! Keep it in an air-tight container like a zip-lock baggie and it will be fun to play with for a long time.

Note: Keep it off of carpet or upholstered furniture, as it could stain.

How to Make Goop

"The Thingmaker" (by Mattel) is another cross-linked chemical toy. What you do is pour a "monster" solution into bug and monster-shaped molds, then set them in ice until gelled. You can make your own "things" with the following recipe, using cookie cutters, etc. as the molds.

To make your own "monster" solution you will need:

4 envelopes unflavored gelatin
8 ounces hot water
1 ounce glycerin (available at the drug store)
Food coloring
non-stick cooking spray

What to do:
Dissolve gelatin in hot water. Add glycerin. Then add the food coloring. Pour into molds that have been sprayed with vegetable oil or cooking spray. Set in refrigerator or freezer and wait 15 minutes or so for the gel to set. Then remove the

creatures from your molds. Careful -- goop creatures can tear fairly easily.

You can also reuse the Goop as often as you wish: place your creations in a tin can and put the tin can into some hot water until the gel becomes liquid. Then it can be poured into new molds.

Smoking Fingertips!

Needed:
Paper match book (safety matches)
tinfoil pie plate
match

What to do:
Tear the striking
surface off of a
paper match book.
Place it face down
in the pie plate,
then light it until
completely burned.
After it cools
thoroughly, there
should be a dark

red residue on the pan. Rub your forefinger and thumb tips in
the residue, then run your finger and thumb together. Wisps
of smoke will rise from your fingers. Try it in the dark, and
you will see a greenish glow.

What happened: The residue from the striking surface
contains red phosphorus, which helps to ignite the safety
matches when they are scraped across it. The red phosphorus
oxidizes at the low temperature caused by the friction
between your thumb and finger.

Cartesian Divers !

Needed:

An empty 2 liter bottle with cap

water

Your "Diver" *(this can be many different things – what you need is something that can hold a bubble of air in it, such as: the bulb from an eyedropper; the cap from a ball point pen; small test tube; plastic straw; a sealed plastic packet of lemon juice or soy sauce from a restaurant, etc. – experiment with different items!)*

A weight for the diver: small dab of clay, play dough, paper clip, etc.

What to do:

Fill your 2 liter bottle full of water. Use a small ball of modeling clay to weigh down the open, bottom end of your diver so that it just barely floats in the water. Do this in the sink so you won't have your diver sinking to the bottom of your bottle while you are making adjustments. You want to keep a little air bubble inside it. You can also use a paper clip or two to weigh it down.

Place the diver inside the bottle and make sure it is full to overflowing with water. Screw on the cap. When you squeeze the bottle, the diver should descend.

Why does it do that?

As the bottle is squeezed, the water is forced into the diver. The tiny bit of air in the diver is compressed, the overall density of the diver is increased, and it sinks.

You might also try breaking the heads off three or four wooden matches and try the matchsticks. The air bubbles trapped in the splintered wood make the match heads act as cartesian divers.

You can make a game out of your diver by fashioning a paper clip "hook" on the bottom of the diver, and placing a wight with a similar hook on the bottom of your bottle. Try to get your diver to "hook" onto the weight if you can.

Fighting for Space !

When you pour water out of a bottle, it makes a gurgling sound. This is because air is entering the bottle to replace the water you have poured out. If the neck of the bottle is very narrow, air cannot enter the bottle easily – the water coming out is fighting for space with the air going in the narrow neck. In fact, if the hole is very small, the water will not come out at all. So let's try it!

Needed:
jelly jar with metal screw-on cap or lid
small nail
hammer
water

What to do:
With the hammer and nail, make a small hole in the metal lid of your jar. Now fill your jar with water and put the cap on securely. Hold the jar upside down. You'll see that the water will not drip out. The hole is too small for both the air and water to use at the same time.

Now, take the lid off again and make a second hole an inch or so from the first one. Put it back on the jar and turn it upside down. This time, water will come out of one hole only, while air enters through the other hole – no more "fighting"!

Soaked Rocks!

Some rocks let water go through them. These are called porous rocks. Non-porous rocks do not let water pass through. Do you think bricks or stones are porous or non-porous? Let's find out!

Needed:
two shallow trays
some large stones or pebbles
water
brick
ruler

What to do:
Place your brick in one tray and the stones or pebbles in the other. Fill each tray with exactly 2″ of water (use your ruler to measure the depth). Let both trays sit for an hour, then come back and measure the water depth in each tray again. What do you find?

The water around the pebbles will look pretty much the same, but the water in the brick tray will be much lower. Bricks are made of baked clay, and clay is porous. There are tiny holes between the particles of baked clay, through which water can move.

If you went on soaking the brick in water, all the holes in the brick would become full of water eventually, and the brick would not be able to soak up any more water.

Whew! We are all experimented out!

That's
The End
...for now!
See you again soon!

If your kids enjoyed our mascots in this book, they'll **love** the coloring book! Get it today!

Illustrated by Jess Erskine

Available on Amazon.com
& other online booksellers everywhere!

Made in the USA
Lexington, KY
23 November 2016